The Depths of a Clam

THE DEPTHS
OF A CLAM

Poems by
Kim Kwang-Kyu

Translated by
Brother Anthony of Taizé
& Kim Young-Moo

Korean Voices Series, Volume 9

WHITE PINE PRESS • BUFFALO, NEW YORK

WHITE PINE PRESS
P.O. Box 236, Buffalo, New York 14201
www.whitepine.org

First Edition

Publication of this book was made possible, in part,
with public funds from the
New York State Council on the Arts, a State Agency,
and the National Endowment for the Arts,
which believes a great nation deserves great art,
and with the generous support of
The Korea Literature Translation Institute
and the Sunshik Min Endowment
for the Advancement of Korean Literature
at the Korea Institute, Harvard University.

Printed and bound in the United States of America.

10-digit ISBN 1-893996-43-3
13-digit ISBN 978-1-893996-43-4

Library of Congress Control Number: 2005929018

CONTENTS

THE HEART OF KŬNAKSAN (1986)

LIKE SOMEONE FUSSING AND FRETTING (1988)

WHEN FIRST WE MET (2003)

INTRODUCTION

When Kim Kwang-Kyu published his first poems in 1975, a noted Korean critic, Yu Jŏng-Ho, commented on the novelty and challenge they represented within the context of Korean lyric poetry. Western readers of these translations will perhaps not immediately realize how revolutionary such poems were in the Korean literary world of the 1970s. The mainstream of Korean verse was at that time dominated by often florid and puzzling expressions of intensely private emotion couched in mainly recondite language with fragmented grammar that was felt to heighten the note of sometimes incoherent ecstasy. The main literary influences received from the West were those known as Symbolism and Modernism. In reaction against this, from early in the 1960s a group of poets inspired by the poet and critic Kim Su-Yŏng had begun searching for ways of writing poems employing more natural language and more closely related to the tensions and conflicts confronting society. The tension between the aesthetic and the social dimensions of literature has long been strongly felt in Korean literary circles. In the years of Japanese annexation 1910-1945 as well as of the military dictatorships that Korea has endured, the aestheticizing approach to literature naturally enough enjoyed official approval.

It may seem strange to Western readers that irony and humor had rarely or never been used in Korean poetry before Kim Kwang-Kyu. It is certain that his familiarity with the works of Brecht and Eich and other German poets was formative from the very beginning of his literary career. He explains that it was only when he discovered how accessible the simple vocabulary and grammatically coherent language of modern German poetry was, that he realized he could write poetry in Korean without having to imitate other Korean poets. In that sense, he can be said to have finally written the "poetry in ordinary language" that Kim Su-Yŏng had called for but not been able to write before his tragic death in an accident in 1968.

In 1973, only a few years before Kim Kwang-Kyu's first poems appeared, Shin Kyŏng-Nim's revolutionary *Farmers' Dance* had been published. It became famous when it received the first Manhae Award in 1974 and served as the spark that ignited a fierce critical debate on the place and proper forms of poetry. It has radically different origins from the work of Kim Kwang-Kyu, being rooted in the language and the life of Korea's rural and urban poor. Whereas Kim Kwang-Kyu had studied in Korea's most prestigious university and read widely in foreign literature, Shin had spent years as a manual laborer and traveling merchant. Many of his poems speak with a plural "we," indicating that they express a widely shared experience of oppression and pain.

Kim Kwang-Kyu recalls how he was first encouraged to write by the laughter of his school friends late in his middle-school days. His earliest writing was witty and his teacher at that time, the poet Cho Pyŏng-Hwa encouraged him to develop his talent in that direction. In contrast, the poetry of Shin Kyŏng-Nim is dark, full of the pain caused by war, social injustice and uprootedness. Korean fiction too is still today rarely amusing; writers tend to favor explorations of pain and alienation in their search for an emotional impact. Tears, not smiles, are the usual criteria for literary success.

The delicate humor with which Kim Kwang-Kyu wrote poems indirectly mocking the military regimes of the '70s and '80s and pinpointing the social problems confronting the rapidly modernizing Korea, delighted thoughtful young intellectuals who could not express plainly what they felt about the military's oppression of human freedom and dignity in their land. At the same time, they deeply appreciated the fact that Kim Kwang-Kyu did nothing to promote himself. His writing was always humble; the poet never put himself forward in a search for fame or recognition. He did not try to become part of any particular group of writers with a shared agenda. Indeed, he firmly refused to join any of the coteries favored by the other poets and writers of his time, with whose work he felt no sympathy whatever. His resolute independence from any kind of literary clique makes him a model of artistic freedom in a country where most younger poets feel obliged to seek membership of a group centered on this or that famed senior writer, surrendering their independence in so doing.

It can be said with certainty that while no Korean poet has ever influenced Kim Kwang-Kyu in his fundamental options of style and subject matter, his writing has had a profound influence on all the young poets who grew up and began to write after he started to publish. His work served to show them the value of stylistic simplicity, the way humor can be used in serious writing, the possibility of talking of social issues while remaining deeply personal. His work was read by them with deep interest precisely because he was clearly not intent on gathering followers or forming a school. The poems came to them as objects freely offered, arising from the poet's life but once published not asking their readers to focus on their author. Thanks to Kim Kwang-Kyu, Korean poetry has become far less arcane and self-centered, and far more interesting for ordinary readers.

When a young professor in the English Department of Seoul National University, Kim Young-Moo, published a selection from his early work in 1988, it was done in recognition of the role Kim Kwang-Kyu had played in sustaining hope during the long years of dictatorship and repression that were at last slowly coming to an end.

Kim Young-Moo died in November 2001. What follows is drawn from the critical intro-duction he wrote for the 1991 Forest Books edition of Kim Kwang-Kyu's earlier poems, based on the essay he had included in his 1988 selection.

* * *

Kim Kwang-Kyu has been heard to say that he normally writes his poems in the morning. Of course, he means quite literally that he usually writes his poems before lunch, but at the same time it seems to suggest that one of the main qualities of his writing is the clear-sighted sensitivity of a freshly wak-ened mind. Kim Kwang-Kyu's poems are trimmed and polished in the morning light after a proper amount of sleep, and an adequate breakfast, they are the fruit of a calm and steady consciousness. In words written for the cover of his first collection of poems (1979) he says, "One of the rights of life, a right that cannot be withheld, is to see and hear and think and speak reality as it is." That suggests that life should not be "a pleasant state of anesthesia" but "a waking pain." The poem carefully written with morning's clear mind is designed to make clear the true character of the state of anesthesia in which the manipulated and regimented consciousness is at home, and invites readers to feel a pain that awakens from that state of unreal fantasy.

A useful introduction to his poetry might be one his very earliest poems, "Spirit Mountain." We may read this as a poem about the birth of a clear mind awakening from the falsehood of the world of ideals and dreams, all the yearning and nostalgia that we tend to experience in connection with childhood and home as well as anything essential and authentic. As we read this poem, that develops so serenely with its "I" carefully controlling feelings and betraying no emotions or thoughts, we are attentive to reflect in turn whether we too do not somehow suffer from a similar painful loss of a childhood home and its mysterious landscapes.

At the center of the poem stands the mysterious mountain that is somehow there without being there, not visible yet glimpsed, not climbable yet present, and we are invited to perceive in the poem both the nature of the mountain and the mind which it continues to haunt. At one level there is a process of discovery; the spirit mountain is not located in space; it is no use taking a bus and going back to a place that is no longer there, for the mystery of the mountain has to be sought at other levels. The poem certainly does not report a simple loss of illusions; it does invite us to re-examine our evaluations of past experience.

In many of Kim Kwang-Kyu's poems we find this theme of "no return," often linked to the home and to childhood, but reported with something other than nostalgia. There is at the same time a feeling that the present has betrayed the past, that if the "unfamiliar people" in the village deny the presence of the spirit mountain now, it is not that they are closer to the truth, but that they have fallen victim to the many forms of alienation present in contemporary society. The village home becomes the symbol of a polluted and shattered national identity.

Pollution and death are everywhere sensed and reported, so that this collection offers an impressive self-portrait of a society in which everyone is reduced, diminished to dwarfish and sub-human proportions. The dominant tone is not a sentimental regret for the past, but a dark satire of the dehumanizing results of those processes which the public authorities often term "modernization." As we leave our boring jobs and trail homewards, we find ourselves compared to cold-blooded reptiles that in the evening return back to their swamp.

It is one of the achievements of Kim Kwang-Kyu's poems that they have made many aware of the deeper roots of the frequently criticized attitudes of selfishness and compromise that seem at first sight to characterize the modern urban mentality. He explores in his poems topics that are more often the subject of novels and short stories than of lyric verse; here we find the selfish philistinism glimpsed in multiple moments of tiny gestures that strike home. In the end, the "general reader" is forced to admit that these portraits are only too familiar.

The basic characteristic of the suffocating social atmosphere Koreans experienced from the early 1970s into the 1990s is a constant repetition of merciless violence. Everywhere we look, we find images of a jungle full of a violence that knows no pity: conscience, ideology, exculpation, regret all equally set aside, the cicada is gobbled up by the spider, the long-prepared beautiful voice silenced in a flash by violence and fear. This reality is clearly expressed in many concrete and telling images. Even the cloudless autumn sky of which Koreans are traditionally so proud becomes a symbol and a source of nothing more than trembling anxiety. Purity can so easily be a mere absence of all the irregularities and variety that go to make up a truly human society.

The responsibilities are as clearly indicated as they can be; the baby crab that tries to return to the "freedom of the sea" is mercilessly crushed by an army truck; "I wonder who" has stifled all the normal activities of people in a happy free society; the riddling image of the dictator is quite transparent. Yet there is always the hope of resistance to the powers of silence and death; the cactus finally blooms after a long restless stay in the dark.

For it is life that triumphs here; the cancer cells within us too are welcomed as part of life, time is spent at night thinking of names for an unborn baby. The struggle against silence and death, the quest for freedom and hope only become more intense, not in a belief that there are always free spirits struggling in spite of oppression and darkness, but *because* of the surrounding darkness. Hope does not come after despair, but arises because despair presents itself as a possibility and is rejected. What we cannot reject or avoid is the fact of time, of aging and final death; it is insofar as we recognize that our life's course is marked by that finality that we are enabled to create something utterly beautiful. Otherwise we fall asleep, back into anesthesia. We cannot escape the fact that the lilac blooms on a rubbish dump, the lotus flower springs from black slime. Even death itself is best understood as the fate of the seed out of which the new flowers spring.

Real life may not be possible in the daily life of present society, but running up into the unblemished nature of a fictitious K'ŭnak Mountain is not at all the solution, for nothing changes there. Nature and human existence follow different laws and values. In nature there are no conflicts of values, but mere being, followed by non-being, and that may be an envious state but what makes life truly human cannot be found there. All that can happen is that the meaning of freedom and nature in human life may, indeed should, be gained by contact with those realities recognized among stones and animals and trees.

Thus the conclusion of these poems for modern humanity is that it is within the present reality that another, dreamed-of reality of freedom and truth has to be constructed by choice and by struggle. And the unfrivolous normality of this vision, Kim Kwang-Kyu's acute discernment as he eagerly examines with eye and ear the stuff of human life, gives us poems in which we encounter a morning mind quite free of all the fumes of anesthesia.

*   *   *

Those words by Kim Young-Moo were written about the poems found in Kim Kwang-Kyu's first three volumes but in many respects they remain true of his more recent work, too. Kim Kwang-Kyu is an extremely consistent writer and he himself admits to a desire to remain faithful to himself, seeing no point in change for its own sake. He reckons that the choices he made at the start of his poetic career remain as valid as ever.

Of course, with the end of military dictatorship and the free election of civilian presidents in the early 1990s, and the corresponding abolition of most forms of censorship together with the repressive security apparatus, one major context for his writing vanished. As a result, we find him turning increasingly to the challenges arising from modern urban life. Already in the 1980s, he was expressing an early awareness of environmental issues and his poetry was always notable for its attention to what is now often termed "the quality of life." Perhaps most noticeable in recent years has been his growing interest in the theme of human mortality. He sees this as an inevitable result of growing older. Many poems look forward to death as a theme allowing him to ponder on questions about the "meaning of human life" and the fundamental values by which people live. He willingly describes himself as a humanist writer; his essential concern is with the value of each individual and his struggle is to enable people to realize more clearly the social and cultural forces that today threaten their humanity.

Explicit questions of religion rarely figure in his work although there are a few poems which evoke the possible existence of a transcendent Being, signs of whose presence in the world are few and fleeting. For the most part, the poet prefers to give expression to a slightly sardonic view of the general limits of human self-awareness, and hints at longings for a more compassionate, affectionate world in which people could live out their allotted life-span a little more meaningfully and happily. He certainly expresses negative attitudes toward the affluent and suggests that the poor are in the end blessed; but he also knows that modern society offers no comfort to the weak and to the elderly.

The resolute simplicity of Kim Kwang-Kyu's poetry is the result of his decision to place content far ahead of form in his scale of values. He shuns every artificial device by which he might give a falsely "poetic" tonality to his verse. Instead, he remains wedded to the epigrammatic tradition, in which the poetry results from the elegant skill with which simple experiences and important notions are expressed. His is an intellectual poetry, with each poem firmly committed to the affirmation of a humanistic vision of the world. Readers may need to be warned that the first-person speaker in his poems should not be too quickly identified with the poet himself. There is so natural a feel to the life stories and 'confessions' that many poems contain that the confusion is easily made. The speaker of many poems is rather a modern Everyman expressing in various ways the alienation and the bewilderment caused by modern city life.

The alienation is very often expressed through an ironic contrast between the present and the past, between nature and society, or between the rural and the urban. In many poems Kim Kwang-Kyu refers to childhood memories of another, seemingly more human Korea in which, despite poverty, people were more attentive to each other and to fundamental values. This enables many Korean readers to sense his concerns very directly, for modernization and urbanization are such recent phenomena that the majority of the poet's own generation were born in rural villages before moving to the cities with their parents in the 1970s or '80s. Yet as Kim Young-Moo wrote, there is no sentimental nostalgia here, no deliberate attempt to romanticize childhood memories; but certainly a major strategy in Kim Kwang-Kyu's work involves establishing contrasts that include notions of a lost Paradise. To that extent it would be possible to see in his world view versions of an ongoing Fall, a process of degeneration that the poet sometimes terms "a return to the swamp." Yet beneath his poems, illuminated by the gentle humor, there shines a glimmer of hope in a redemption—a sense that things do not necessarily have to be as bad as they are, that humanity has a possibility of making other choices, following other priorities.

One stylistic feature of Kim Kwang-Kyu's poetry that soon becomes apparent is his liking for poems that end with a question: "Who am I?" "What tombs will poets leave?" "Who knows where he went?" "What did you do?" This takes us back to the topic of the kind of poetry Kim Kwang-Kyu is writing. His poems are not presented as finished products, works of art designed to be framed and admired. Rather they set out to provoke, to share a disquieting question, awaken readers to troublesome aspects of life. The reader who comes to these poems is thus being invited to wake up from mindless slumber and start thinking about things that matter. These poems are worth translating because the things that matter to Kim Kwang-Kyu matter to everyone, no matter where they live, if they care about staying human.

HISTORICAL NOTE

A short note on Korea's modern history may be necessary for non-Korean readers. Some of Kim Kwang-Kyu's poems refer, directly or indirectly, to these events.

August 15, 1945, the day of the Japanese surrender, is celebrated as National Liberation Day in Korea. For thirty-six years, since its brutal annexation in 1910, Korea had been ruled by Japan. The Japanese surrender at the end of the Second World War was expected to restore independence to the Korean Peninsula. The following Cold War soon led to the horrors of the Korean War (1950-3), which ended with the division of the Korean Peninsula into North and South by the "Demilitarized Zone" roughly following the 38th parallel.

When the first president of the Republic of Korea (South Korea), Syngman Rhee, tried to manipulate a third term in office in 1960, the students of high-schools and universities took to the streets in peaceful protest demonstrations, and on April 19 of that year many were brutally massacred.

Syngman Rhee fell, but then General Park Chung-hee took power in a military coup d'état in May 1961, crushing all hope of democratic government. Under President Park the most dreaded social force was the notorious Korean CIA, a secret police force responsible for much repression, torture and violence. His government pursued a vigorous policy of industrialization, encouraging millions of young people to leave their rural villages to look for work in the burgeoning factories and sweatshops of the rapidly expanding cities. Correspondingly, increasing numbers of city-dwellers found white-collar jobs in offices of every kind, as Seoul in particular grew to be one of the world's largest cities.

After 1971, when President Park rewrote the Constitution ("The Yushin Reform") to make himself president for life, opposition and repression both grew. In October 1979, President Park was assassinated by the head of the KCIA, for reasons which have never been made clear. For a few months, it seemed that free democracy might be restored.

Again, the military imposed its will, and the rise of General Chun Doo-Hwan culminated in a coup in May 1980, coinciding with the murderous repression of a popular struggle for democracy in the city of Kwangju. Again all opposition was violently repressed, speech controlled, the press gagged.

April and May have special significance in Korea, linked as they are to the hopes frustrated in the 1960s, all through the 1970s and the 1980s. The earlier poems of Kim Kwang-Kyu were written under presidents Park and Chun, and they represent a courageous challenge to the officially-approved attitudes of submission and silence. At the same time, the materialistic, self-centered culture of the modern world was slowly taking control of the main cities and of people's lifestyles while working life for the majority meant the boredom of meaningless office work or poorly paid manual labor. The unquestioning attitude of many is challenged in many poems that distinguish Kim Kwang-Kyu as Korea's foremost social satirist.

The Last Dream to Affect Us
(1979)

Spirit Mountain

In my childhood village home there was a mysterious mountain. It was called Spirit Mountain. No one had ever climbed it.

By day, Spirit Mountain could not be seen.
With thick mist shrouding its lower half and clouds that covered what rose above, we could only guess dimly where it lay.

By night, too, Spirit Mountain could not be seen clearly.
In the moonlight and starlight of bright cloudless nights its dark form might be glimpsed, yet it was impossible to tell its shape or its height.

One day recently, seized with a sudden longing to see Spirit Mountain—it had never left my heart—I took an express bus back to my home village. Oddly enough, Spirit Mountain had utterly vanished and the unfamiliar village folk I questioned swore that there was no such mountain there.

Ars Poetica

A dog stops suddenly
as it aimlessly wanders across an empty square
through the hard light of a summer noontide.
Reaching its ears

from high on crowded concrete crosses
on vineyard slopes
sweetly unfolding out of light and water comes

a sound

left at the bottom of the sea while the fish—
now corpses in the fish-market—
stare up at us wordlessly.
All those many fishes' despairing names—

not the borrowed names we use for a time,
not a promise, and unable to record
even the twittering of a sparrow,
always stripped off, thrown down, crumpled,

inadequate clothing of sounds . . .
language!

Our mother tongue,
clustered thick with consonants,
is quite worn out before we can use it,
so that anyone who lives with language
fearless and unsorrowing,
not looking for any blessing

but only pursuing the sounds
that can never be spoken,
treading in the footsteps of the wind,
keeps repeating vain despair.

Being and Non-Being (I)

The red bricks of the dye store,
soaked by springtime rainfall,
take on a strange tint found in no color-chart.

That tint, that no one takes note of,
lingers briefly on roof and walls
then slips away from the house again.

A sharp-eyed pigeon flies
up after that tint as if it were something
that might be seen and caught,
up into the haze where chimes echo.

At last the flying pigeon returns exhausted,
perches on the TV antenna of the house next door and
stares down vacantly at the brick building messy with dye.

Being and Non-Being (II)

It vaguely wandered far off just above the horizon, then spun around me, very close by.

Fluttering like a butterfly it settled on my shoulder, scurrying away like a squirrel when I stealthily reached up a hand, then when I ran panting after it, it suddenly penetrated inside me, constricting my breast.

Once I clung hold of something that had come close beside me. Something cold-blooded and slithery like a snake writhed in my hand, trying to escape. Like in a wrestling match we grappled this way and that but finally it got away. For it had no trunk or head or limbs or wings and could not be seen.

It kept following me and all the time I kept pursuing it.

Sometimes I came across it in a bookstore but on inspection it would turn out to be just a book. Occasionally I glimpsed it in the market or in a store but what I seized would turn out to be a fish or a fruit or a suit or some such-like object. Once I saw it walking along in the shape of a smartly dressed middle-aged man and followed him but he was just a run-of-the-mill insurance-office clerk. I hastened to examine a place brightly lit up at night but it was only a petro-chemical complex operating non-stop.

At last I discovered it in a hitherto unknown alleyway that I had entered by chance. It was at the back of a seedy house I felt I had often seen some-where before—a messy spot to one side of a half-sunlit storage terrace with worn-out pieces of furniture strewn around and a chimney standing askew in one corner.

Emerging from that alleyway I was surprised to see it among passers-by and cars and trees and cigarette-kiosks and roadside pushcarts. It seemed to be visible everywhere in the world.

But when I tried to grasp it, it was nowhere at all to be found.

I

Come to think of it,
I am
my father's son
my son's father
my older brother's younger brother
my younger brother's older brother
my wife's husband
my sister's brother
my uncle's nephew
my nephew's uncle
my teacher's pupil
my pupil's teacher
my country's tax-payer
my neighborhood's army reservist
my friend's friend
my enemy's enemy
my doctor's patient
my regular bar's customer
my dog's master
my household's family head

therefore
I am a
son
father
younger brother
older brother
husband
brother
nephew
uncle
pupil
teacher
tax-payer
army reservist

friend
enemy
patient
customer
master
family head—
not just
one I.

Tell me then:
what is that I
that no one knows—
and this I
standing here now—
who am I?

Requiem

Perhaps he never existed to begin with?
So I reflected as I stood beside the sea
at the crack of dawn watching an hour-glass run
and sometimes as I paused before a red light
at a level-crossing.
No.
He definitely existed.
His clothes hanging beside the window
waving in the breeze,
his glasses laid askew on the desk,
five stubbed-out cigarette-ends
were left behind,
as well as half a bottle of his favorite liquor.
Perhaps he has gone away,
casting off expressions, voice and gestures,
finally even his body?
Perhaps we are left behind here
after seeing him off?
No.
He has suddenly gone inside,
leaving his shoes at the door,
vanished inside memory.
Then are we outside?
Perhaps we are lingering outside
looking for him?
No need for that.
Nothing can conceal him now
or hide us.
He exists in most vivid form
inside.
Don't think of him.
Look at him.

Epitaph

He never read a line of poetry,
not one single novel.
He lived happily all his life,
earned a lot of money,
rose to high position
and left this magnificent tombstone
for which some famous literary figure
wrote an epitaph eulogizing him.
Even if the world is reduced to ashes
this stone will firmly resist the heat
of the flames and survive
to become a precious historical document.
Then what on earth does history record?
What tombs will poets leave?

Going Home in the Evening

We gave up any thought of flying long ago.

These days we don't even try to run.
We dislike walking, so we try to ride.
We mostly travel by bus or subway.
Once on board, we all try to get a seat.
Once seated, we lean back snoozing.
Not that we are tired,
but every time money-making is over
our heads become atrophied
and scales sprout all over our bodies.
Our blood has grown cold
but still, with our eyes half-open
our practiced feet take us home.

We return every evening to our homes
like reptiles returning to their swamp.

Today

When the sound of chimes rings out from the church
I get up, throw open the window,
draw in deep refreshing breaths.
Ah! That sweet odor of lead—the exhaust fumes
floating through the early morning air!
Health is truly a gift of God.
As I duly eat my morning rice
with mercury-whitened bean-sprout soup,
then ride to work on a crowded bus,
I always love today especially.
Today is the day I have to pay the month's installment
to the building and loans society.

At nine o'clock, feeling
the prickly glare of instruments, I stand
before a daily growing metal mass.
Suddenly emerging from the metal, a cricket's chirp
or a frog's croak,
coming from this metal so utterly incapable of error,
sometimes makes me feel sinful.
How can I be asked to be sorry
for forty years lived according to Safety First?
I must pray, saying: I repent.

With thick glasses shielding bloodshot eyes,
today as usual I rummage in trashcans
searching among cigarette-ends and crumpled doodles
and inside crushed soft-drinks cans
for conspiracies hidden there.
All day long I carefully rummage through the trash
and if I cannot find anything
my heart grows more anxious still, for
who could believe in a world without conspiracies?

An annual interest of 10% maturing in 15 years . . .

I spend the day absorbed in calculating costs
then in the evening I meet my friends,
smart fellows all together,
winners and losers versus today,
drinking so as not to get drunk,
making uproar so as not to talk
driven out by the midnight curfew,
making our way home,
bringing up what we have eaten
beside an alley-way telegraph pole,
briefly weeping tears clear as liquor
as we gaze up at the hazily shining stars.

In this treeless village, once the television is finished
we each and all give the house over to the dogs
and sleep each others' sleep snoring virile snores.
With pitiful gestures we dream daytime dreams
where it's even ok to look angry:
—You bastards! just you show your faces quick!
(It's even ok to swear)
—You bastards! speak up quick!
Just think for once!
Who's the boss around here?
The things that we hear in dreams,
that the ear gets used to hearing there,
are things we forget
every time we wake up.

Faint Shadows of Old Love

In late 1960, the year of the April Revolution,
we met at five in the afternoon,
happily clasped hands in greeting
then sitting in a chill unheated room,
our breaths condensing white,
we engaged in heated discussions.
Foolishly enough we believed
we were living for the sake of something,
for something that had nothing to do with politics.
The meeting ended inconclusively and that evening,
drinking grog at Hyehwa-dong Rotary,
we worried in a pure-minded way
about problems of love and spare-time jobs
and military service.
Each of us sang as loud as he could
songs no one listened to,
songs no one could imitate.
Those songs we sang for no reward
rose up into the winter sky
and fell as shooting stars.

Eighteen years later we finally met again,
all wearing neckties.
Each of us had become something.
We had become the older generation,
living in dread of revolution.
We chipped in to cover the cost of the party,
exchanged news of our families
and asked the others how much they were earning.
Anxious about the soaring cost of living,
happily deploring the state of the world,
expertly lowering our voices
as we discussed rumors,
we were all of us living for the sake of living.
This time no one sang.

We parted, leaving abundant drink and side dishes behind us,
after noting one another's new phone numbers.
A few went off to play poker.
A few went off to dance.
A few of us walked sadly
along the University Street we used to frequent,
clutching rolled-up calendars under our arms,
in a place we had returned to after long wanderings,
in that place where our former love had bled.
Unfamiliar buildings had appeared suspiciously
though the roadside plane trees stood in their old places
and a few remaining dry leaves trembled there,
sending shudders up our spines.
Aren't you ashamed?
Aren't you ashamed?
As the wind's whisper flowed about our ears
we deliberately made middle-aged talk about our health
and took one step deeper into the swamp.

The Land of Mists

In the land of mists,
always shrouded in mist,
nothing ever happens.
And if something happens
nothing can be seen
because of the mist.
For if you live in mist
you get accustomed to mist
so you do not try to see.
Therefore in the land of mists
you should not try to see.
You have to hear things.
For if you do not hear you cannot live,
so ears keep growing bigger.
People like rabbits
with ears of white mist
live in the land of mists.

A Ghost

Hush!

Look at that black car
speeding through the dark.
Look at those men in everyday clothes
vanishing up side-streets smoking cigarettes.
Look at those oily marks
spreading over the devastated earth.
Look at those pieces of iron
littering every roadside.

If you cannot see the shape of the ghost
you must all be blind!

Within the flying dust and cement
that enter our lungs each time we breathe
until at last it seems we must suffocate

if you cannot hear the voice of the ghost
you must all be deaf!

Hear the voice of those corpses
rotting sunk in some deep pond.
Hear the voice of those broken bodies
that rise smoking from every chimney and fill the sky.
Hear the groans that to the bitter end
do not emerge from mouths clenched tightly shut.
Hear those shouted commands that rise
from a treeless sandy plain.

Hush!

Conversation Drill

(In the land of mists I wanted to make friends with many people. I also wanted
to bargain for low prices when I was buying things. But my words failed com-
pletely to get across. The reason was my ignorance of the following basic con-
versation pattern.)

No.
That's wrong.
I disagree.

Yes Sir.
That's right Sir.
I agree Sir.

Of course.
You must always agree.
It is not possible to disagree with me.
In your dictionary the word disagree does not exist
and in my dictionary the word agree does not exist.

So we use the same words
but our dictionaries are different Sir.
I will be more careful in future Sir
and before you disagree I will agree.

Between Ideas

Now if
a poet thinks of nothing but poems
a politician thinks of nothing but politics
a businessman thinks of nothing but business
a worker thinks of nothing but labor
a judge thinks of nothing but law
a soldier thinks of nothing but war
an engineer thinks of nothing but factories
a farmer thinks of nothing but farming
a civil servant thinks of nothing but administration
a scholar thinks of nothing but study

it may seem that the world will become a paradise
but in actual fact

if there is not someone thinking of the relation

between poems and politics
between politics and business
between business and labor
between labor and the law
between the law and war
between war and factories
between factories and farming
between farming and administration
between administration and study

then nothing but
scrap paper and
power and
money and
exploitation and
prisons and
ruins and
pollution and

pesticides and
repression and
statistics

will remain.

Almanac

When spring comes they will awake.
Stretching, they will try to rise.
Prevent them from rising.
Teach them how sweet
a morning bed is.

Tidy up neatly those hills
where rocks lie scattered in disorder;
plant only trees that can be used for lumber
and make them grow straight.

Make them happy with the early summer breezes
that bring flowery balm to every scratch that
the branches make as they pass through acacia groves.

By the burning sun of June's month-long drought
make them thirsty;
by the pouring rains of July's month-long monsoon
submerge them in water.

Make the curving meandering rivers
flow in straight lines
and to the child born in the apartment block there,
just above the embankment,
have them fix a number instead of a name.

Frighten them by banks of late-autumn mist
that cover the mountain peaks
and drop down through the pine groves behind the villages.

When winter comes they will feel cold.
Shivering, they will try to draw near the fire.
Stop them getting near.
Tell them that when winter goes spring will come.
Make them hibernate.

Small Men

They are getting smaller.
They keep getting smaller.
Before they had finished growing,
already they had begun to get smaller.
Before they first fell in love, as they thought about war
they began to get smaller.
The older they get the smaller they get.
As they break off a yawn they get smaller.
As they shudder from terrifying nightmares
they get smaller.
Jumping every time someone knocks they get smaller.
Hesitating even at a green light they get smaller.
As they lament that they do not grow old quickly enough
they get smaller.
As they bury their heads in the newspaper,
since the world is so calm they get smaller.
Standing neatly in line wearing ties they get smaller.
As they all think about earning money doing business
they get smaller.
As they listen to inaudible orders they get smaller.
As they repeat words identical as uniforms they get smaller.
As they fight with invisible enemies they get smaller.
As they attend multiple meetings and clap they get smaller.
As they consume luncheons of power and pick their teeth
they get smaller.
As they grow fat and play golf they get smaller.
As they go to cocktail parties and drink scotch they get smaller.
As they embrace their wives now grown too stout they get smaller.

They have grown small.
At last they have grown small.
They have grown smaller than the quick-eyed sparrows
that fly up to the eaves from the garden.
Now they know how to smoke while wearing a mask.
They know how to laugh louder than ever at unfunny moments.

They know how to be sincerely sad for long periods
about things that are not sad.
They know how to keep happiness hidden deep down.
They know how to evaluate correctly each kind of anger.
They know how not to say what they really feel
and to cast furious glances at one another.
They know how not to think of questions nobody asks.
They know how to count their blessings
every time they pass a prison.
They know how each to take an umbrella and walk down alley-ways
when it rains.
Instead of dancing in the plains
they know how to sing falsetto in bars.
When they make love they know how to cut back on uneconomical
wearisome caresses.
Truly,
they have grown small.
They have grown quite small enough.
All that is left is their Name, Occupation and Age.
Now they have grown so small they are invisible.

They cannot get any smaller.

Death of a Baby Crab

One baby crab,
caught with its mother,

while the big crabs, tied together by a straw rope
foam and wave aimless legs,
tumbles out of the hawker's basket
and crawls off sideways, sideways over the roadway,
in quest of past days of hide-and-seek in the mud
and the freedom of the sea.
It pricks up its eyes and gazes all around,
then dies, squashed across the roadway,
run over by a speeding army truck.

No one notices how a light of glory shines
where the baby crab's remains rot in the dust.

Delayed Enlightenment

We were by chance born brothers.
My elder brother
loved to play at soldiers.
He became a general
all covered in medals.
I used to love to paint.
I became a private
painting cobblestones.
Maybe life's like that at times
but soon it's got to change—
that's how I used to think
as I counted the days to discharge.
Our older sister
born to keep us company,
bright as a doll,
became the wife
of a well-to-do company chairman.
I used to like to cry.
I became a worker wearing glasses.
Life is really unknowable
but at least everyone goes his own way—
that's how I used to think
as I waited for the bus that didn't come.
We were all born fellow-countrymen.
Some have become administrators ruling us
or wage-earners faithful like dogs
or housewives taking fish home.
Others have been put into prisons
that their own hands built.
History always changes and
is always the same,
always on the side of the winners,
but there are always more on the losing side.
There's no way you can start all over again
but you can't let it end like this—
that's how I think now.

No, It's Not So
(1983)

An Old, Old Question

Who doesn't know that?
As time flows on
flowers wither
leaves fall
and one day or other
we too grow old and die like animals,
return to the earth,
vanish towards the sky.
Yet the world, unchanging
as we live on, keeps prodding us awake
with an old old question.
Only look!
Isn't this new and amazing and lovely?
Every year the deep perfume
of lilacs growing on mounds of rubbish
fills the back-streets.
An unsightly prickly cactus
dangling from the corner of a broken pot,
blooms with one bright flower
after long restless nights.
The bright form of a lotus flower
springs from a pond's black slime.
And surely
a child's sweet smile,
sprung from a dark human womb,
makes us still more perplexed?
We oblige our children
          to put on shoes
to prevent them treading barefoot on the ground
and when their hands get muddy
we wipe them off saying, "That's dirty."
For goodness sake!
Not rooted in the ground,
their bodies not smeared with mud,
the children's bursting hearts,

their bouncing bodies,
as they frolic and grow,
all that welling energy—
where do you think it comes from?

The Depths of a Clam

After they got married, the girl never confessed her first love affair. And of course her husband never got round to telling his secrets, either. As they went on living, their lives were nothing but disenchantment. In order to conceal their disenchantment, they said countless things, but there were still things they did not say.

The disenchantment built up like lead inside their bodies. The words they could not say hardened in their breasts like cancerous cells.

Although the disenchantment was unavoidable, they always wanted to speak. They longed to pour out all that they had on their hearts to someone. It seemed that if nobody was going to remember, they would be able to relax and tell it all at length.

At times it happened that other people said something similar. Or while reading they would discover a passage to that effect and thankfully underline it. Or they heard music that was more explicit than words. Yet to the very end their lips remained sealed like clams.

Finally, after living long years in unending disenchantment, they died still treasuring their secrets. In so far as they were silent, history was concealed and truth was hidden. So today, as we repeat their life and discern those hidden depths, we still believe that this world is worth living in.

Mount Inwang

Majestic Mount Inwang!
In old days a breeding-place of tigers
and for five hundred years rising
on the outskirts of the nation's capital—
then called Hanyang—
gazing down on the joys and sorrows
of Seoul as if on childhood toys.
The home of my remote grandfather
Where now is the trustworthy face
of that tremendous rocky slide
I used to itch to climb when I was a child?
Today broken glass and plastic bags lie scattered
in the pine groves of the steep valley
where pure water used to run between the rocks.
A gray oily haze shimmers
veiling the mountain's mass
and now its mighty spurs,
crisscrossed in all directions with asphalt roads,
imprisoned in the midst of a population of eight million,
seem about to collapse,
panting and gasping for breath,
showing only a desiccated profile,
a shabby back,
slumped down on one edge of downtown Seoul,
reduced in old age to life in a rented room.
Poor Mount Inwang!

To the Korean Bear

Is there anything new under the sun?
Creation too is nothing more than an effect.
In the beginning there was a cause
followed by an effect.
That effect in turn became a cause
and that cause once again gave birth to an effect.
Old cause and effect were replaced
by new cause and effect,
until at last they arrived at today.
In which case yesterday is today's cause
and today is yesterday's effect,
while today is tomorrow's cause
and tomorrow is undoubtedly today's effect.
Foolish bear trying to separate cause and effect!
Don't try to manufacture a causeless effect,
calling a new cause an old effect
and an old effect a new cause.
Sometimes even death can become a cause.
And there is nothing new under the sun.

Old Marx

Look, my young friend,
that's not what history is like.
It's not what you think it's like.
It's not something that unfolds dialectically.
Literature too is not like that, either.
It's not what you think it's like.
It's not something that changes logically.
You are young,
it's ok if you still don't know
but just suppose that the moment
you finally realize that really
history and literature are not like that
comes when you have already reached the age
where you can no longer change anything
in your life?
Look, my young friend,
ideology in the head
can never become love in the heart.
Even though our opinions may differ
how fortunate it is
that each one of us lives our share
and how unsatisfying
that each one of us lives only once
then is dead and gone.
Even though we die and become the past,
history remains as the present
and literature honestly records
the complexities of life in days gone by.
Look, my young friend,
take care
that your heart doesn't harden
before your body has had time to grow old.
Take care!

The Birth of a Stone

I wonder if there are stones
in those deep mountain ravines
that no one has ever visited?
I went up the mountain
in quest of a stone no one had ever seen
from the remotest of times.

Under ancient pines
on steep pathless slopes
there was a stone.
I wonder
how long
this stone all thick with moss
has been
here?

Two thousand years? Two million? Two billion?
No.
Not at all.
If really till now no one
has ever seen this stone,
it is only
here
from now on.

This stone
was only born
the moment I first saw it.

Roadside Trees in April

Their tops were cut off long ago
so as not to touch the power lines.
This year even their limbs have been lopped
so they cannot sway if a spring breeze blows
and only the trunks remain like torsos
suffocating and grim.
When the lilac perfume deepens,
memories of another April day return
but now every trailing branch has been cut off
so that the street-side weeping willows,
lined up in rows,
unable even to put out new leaves,
seething with impatience but
unable to utter even a cry,
are putting out leaves from their trunks.

The Garbage-Collectors

You know nothing about us at all.
Of course you think that
with the money we get from collecting garbage
we cover the cost of a glass of spirits on snowy days
and that with three years' savings
we buy a hand-cart and set ourselves up
as dealers in scrap and second-hand junk
but that's not the case.
We are nothing at all like those
who pass giving a few cents' worth of pop-corn
in exchange for old magazines and newspapers,
for discarded empty bottles and even scrap iron,
those who stand guarding the alleys to the world beyond
with an eye on the corpses' gold teeth.
We return burnt coal-briquettes to the soil
on the garbage-tips where dead money is thrown,
the places where all the world's desires end up.
Odd ownerless shoes and bloodstained rags,
stinking fish-bones and strips of split plastic,
all gathering together in a friendly way,
scattering in the wind and soaking in the rain,
set out homewards from the garbage-tip.
We who here on earth's last precipice
burn away the stench of this sickening world,
we are nothing like them at all.
All you who can hear only an idle spring day's languor
in the clacking scissors of junk- and scrap-dealers
and run as far as you can from the garbage-tip
on your way to the bank, .
on your way to church,
you know nothing at all about us.

People I Long to Meet

They are all strangers to me
yet the faces are strangely familiar.
How many familiar strangers there are!
I wonder where we first met?
In the nursery-school garden
where a brood of chicks pecked at feed?
At the country market-place
where we bought and ate cotton-candy?
On a bench in the school playground
newly blooming with acacia-flowers?
Was it sitting under a scorching sun
protesting on the roof of a sewing-factory?
Or being driven like animals
from springtime streets with streaming eyes?
Was it in the little night-guard's room
playing checkers to decide who paid for the drinks?
Or high up on a mountain
pantingly pursuing spies?
Was it in front of a prison at dawn
as we waited for friends?
In a room in an alley-way inn
with bean-curd sellers passing by outside?
Or in the corridor outside a maternity ward,
chain-smoking as we waited?
Was it hawking loads of garlic
round apartment complexes?
Was it in a tax-office filing VAT returns?
Maybe in a suburban cinema
during a civil-defense training session?
Perhaps in some corner seat of a coffee-shop
discreetly handing over money in a white envelope?
Were we waiting to change planes
in some airport transit area?
Was it as we spent the night at a wake
in some house of mourning?

None of those.
They are all lying memories,
false illusions.
We only brushed past each other,
we never really met.
They are all familiar-faced strangers
The strangers I know are very few!

Hope

And the word hope too
strictly speaking
is a foreign word, surely?
Talking about despair
with a friend who came
late one night
soaked with rain
I thought seriously about hope.
He quoted Benjamin,
saying that hope is something
for the despairing,
aping Descartes
with 'I despair
therefore I hope'
but I wonder if what was said
by that Jew driven by despair
to end his life
was wrong?
Hope is decidedly not
for the despairing,
since it is for those
who have not lost hope.
In that case I wonder if we,
discussing hope all night
like hunted Jews,
are already despairing or
have not yet lost hope?
When curfew time ended
he disappeared into the dark,
his bloodshot eyes bright with despair.
Truly hope is always there ahead,
even in hours of despair,
not something that comes from somewhere else,
not something somebody else gives us,
something we get by fighting

and have to defend.
Hope
is certainly no
foreign word.

I Wonder Who

I wonder who has abolished the downtown bus-stops.

I wonder who is blowing a whistle far away
as he follows along behind us
eavesdropping on what we say
spying on our loves,
and has gone off robbing us of our deep sleep.
Our happy home has been raided like a brothel
our laboriously cultivated flowerbeds
trampled underfoot.
I wonder who has dirtied our pure skies
put barbed-wire round our green villages
emptied waste oil into our broad oceans
disturbed our serious meetings
stopped our forceful steps
arrested our honest neighbors.
I wonder who is pointing a gun at our backs
With our eyes blindfolded
our mouths gagged
throats strangling
veins pumped up,
I wonder who has entered our heads
and is sticking a knife into our brains,
reading things we never wrote.
I wonder who is beating a drum far away
as he drives us up a blind alley.

I wonder who is this someone we didn't invite.

Opinions Concerning the Solar Calendar

A year of 365 days,
no matter what you say,
is much too short.
To go on doing the things you have begun
and complete the things you have gone on doing,
no matter what you say,
it's much too short.
If I have power,
if I have the power to control time,
I will at once arrange it so that from now on
the calendar will be corrected
and a New Year come only
once every three years.

(Such were the thoughts of one person
celebrating New Year
while everybody else thought as follows)

A year of 365 days,
no matter what you say,
is much too long.
To go on doing the things you have begun
and complete the things you have gone on doing,
no matter what you say,
it's much too long.
If we have our way,
if we have our way about how the globe turns,
we will at once unite our strength
and arrange it so that from now on
a New Year can come
three times every year,
a new springtime can come
three times every year.

Tricolor flag

In the land of mists, everybody
wanted to become a civil servant.
Once they had become civil servants
they put on black uniforms
and prepared to wield power.
In the end, everyone had become a civil servant
and there were no citizens left
to pay taxes.
They found themselves obliged
to take turns acting as citizens,
just as they did night-duty and late shifts

In the land of mists, everybody
wanted to become a shopkeeper.
Once they had become shopkeepers
they put on yellow uniforms
and prepared to earn money.
In the end everyone had become a shopkeeper
and there were no customers left
to buy things.
They found themselves obliged
to elect customers,
just as they chose chairmen for their associations.

In the land of mists, everybody
wanted to become a soldier.
Once they had become soldiers
they put on green uniforms
and prepared to defend the nation.
In the end everyone had become a soldier
and there were no civilians left to defend.
They found themselves obliged
to reduce the numbers under arms
and enter public service as civilians,
just as they went on night-watch or guard-duty.

(It has only recently been discovered that this has some connection with the black, yellow and green tricolor flag of the land of mists)

To My Children

Never go into dangerous places.
And it is better to do nothing
that might make people suspect you.
That's what my deceased father
always used to say.
Obedient to his words,
I stayed indoors
like a cat on a sunny back porch.
I was always a sweet child—
someone who lives peacefully,
someone who never does anything,
someone who leaves no trace behind.
According to his words, if you live like that
what difficulties can you have in life?
I was willing but it is not so easy
to live like that either.
Maybe it's because I lack mental stamina?
On days typhoons blow,
sitting indoors at home
sorting out dog-eared books
and burning old diaries,
I keep tearing things up
so that nothing will remain.
For suppose something were to remain!
And even if one day suddenly
I became unable to do this,
suppose somebody were to remember me!
But in any case maybe a strange
telephone call will come first.
When an earthquake strikes,
just staying indoors is dangerous too.
Even doing nothing
makes people suspect you.
Having shunned the sin of
the quiet life,

this is what I will tell my children:
Don't live peacefully.
At least do something.
No matter how shameful the trace,
leave something behind you.

No! Not So

All the pain of the leaves
bursting out in anguish
through their hardened shells
and the pain of the blooming azaleas
had become a furious cry
on that day the earth shook
as he raced ahead of the others
then fell near the Blue House.
His satchel was still bulging
with lunchbox and dictionary
as he fell to the roadway,
never to rise again,
robbed of his bright smile
and supple movements.
So did he die in vain
in the twentieth year of his youth?

No.
Not at all.
Since the day he cried: "Drive them out!"'
he has become a lion, eternally young,
roaring fiercely.
On the central campus lawn
he has become a fountain
that rises skywards.
His surviving companions sheepishly
graduated and did their military service,
got married and had children so that
before you knew it today they are
middle-aged wage-earners,
while he has remained unchanging
a young university student
attending lectures regularly
absorbed in impassioned debates
skillfully pursuing the ball.

Look there and see his vital image,
unswervingly following truth
in his proud successor,
defending the nation with his whole being:
our promising son
tending anew those ideals
we had forgotten.

So it is.
Since the day he fell near the Blue House,
endlessly rising again
he races on
ahead of us.

The Heart of K'ŭnaksan
(1986)

Tightropes

There's no audience, yet
everyone's carrying a pole
and walking the tightrope up in the air
where so many ropes are crisscrossed
that if there's no way ahead on one
          they jump across to the next
and even when resting keep switching
from one to another and back.
But if you fall
between the ropes you
vanish
into the unfathomed dark.
With so many ropes crisscrossing
it sometimes looks like solid ground
but if you blink one eye and
make a false step
you've had it so,
trying hard not to fall,
controlling their swaying bodies,
everyone's ever so cautiously
toeing the line.

Pagoda Tree

The local people used to call that tree where every night the owl came and shrieked a pagoda tree.

The pagoda tree cast a broad shadow by the well side. The bucket vanished, a pump appeared; later they introduced a piped water supply, and in that place a short while ago a filling station arose, but still the pagoda tree stands there unchanged.

During the Korean War, the bombed-out wreck of an army truck lay for a long time abandoned beneath the pagoda tree. After any items fit for the scrap dealers had been torn away, it became a plaything for the children and for almost 3 years that great lump of iron lay there rusting red until at last it broke up and disappeared.

A few scraps of shrapnel stuck into the pagoda tree too, but those bits of metal gradually rusted and were absorbed by the sap; finally a gnarl appeared over the spot. At some time or other a nature protection sign was hung there.

When I look at that pagoda tree, still now I long to stroke its great bulk, to lean against it, go climbing up into it, even to become its roots or branches. And whether I'm hurrying along on foot, or in a taxi, whenever I pass before it a feeling of shame arises.

For I keep thinking that motion is what that pagoda tree is doing, while standing fixed in one spot today as of old is what in reality I myself am doing.

Before an Old Incense Burner

Were those days really different from now?
Everyone is ready to admire a well-turned, well-shaped,
pretty incense burner
and treasure it lovingly
but this is no exquisitely beautiful
lidded incense burner in inlaid celadon
giving a glimpse of the clouds and lotus flowers
of 800 years ago.
It is one that came cracked and twisted from the kiln.
Incense was never once burned in it;
it just lay kicking around in some potter's shed
and precisely this one ugly squarish pot
that endured all that time
and has survived until today
holds all the skies of ancient Koryŏ
within its battered form.

April-May

I'm not sure when it began
but every year now April only comes
and doesn't go.
Azaleas and forsythias bloom everywhere
and as the scent of lilac strengthens,
the torn and faded banner flaps again
and the old wound in my side throbs,
all my bruised bones ache separately
and from the dry black wound
blood flows again.
Relapse or resurrection, I wonder?
The acacias bloom gloriously
and one day sad with the cuckoo's call
along the banks between green sprouting rice-fields
women pass bearing a coffin
while from rubbish dumps in woods or at roadsides
bodies denied even a shroud rise up
unsleeping,
unrotting,
unforgotten.
Time only thickens.
I'm not sure when it began
but every year now May only comes
and doesn't go.

The Summer There Were No Cicadas

One cicada was singing in a persimmon tree
then flew off but was abruptly checked in mid-air—
aha, a spider's web spreading wide!
The spider hiding under the edge of the roof
had the struggling cicada tied up in a flash,
no point in mentioning anything like
conscience or ideas,
no place for regret or excuses.
At the end of seven years' training,
the cicada's lovely voice
ended up after scarcely seven days
as a spider's supper.
If you're caught like that, you've had it.
The cicadas stopped singing
and flying.
It was a remarkably long hot summer.

Wisdom Tooth

It's a nuisance.
It ought to come out.
It will just go rotten
and damage the molars.
A wisdom tooth should come out.
I don't know why they grow at all,
you can't chew with them.
(A doctor's words are always
medically correct).
But will taking it out
really be the cure?
(Frightened patients
are invariably pig-headed)
I think I will not get rid
of this wretched tooth
though its aching keeps me awake at night.
It may be a bothersome wisdom tooth
but who if not I will chew on
and be capable of patiently enduring
and treasuring
this part of myself
that gives me my share of pain?

People on the Bus

Fumes of tear-gas rise
from young people carrying books.
When they pass through university areas,
the people on the bus
wipe their eyes
and sneeze.
But though their noses run,
they say not a word,
They too used to go to school,
now they have done military service,
they pay their taxes,
raise their families,
they are ordinary citizens
struggling through life;
those things the young dislike
they are none too fond of either
but they are just grown-ups with dirty hands,
unable to have a natural opinion
about square-shaped things.
So those who get on the bus
amidst shouted slogans
and hurtling stones,
dodging volleys of tear-gas bombs,
their mouths still covered with handkerchiefs,
they are no mere idle on-lookers,
they are not unconcerned passers-by,
Their names are unknown but
who are these oh so familiar people?

Going Up Over Bukhan Hill

If you go up the road over Bukhan hill,
in valleys thick with trees and bushes
where the mountain-birds sing sweetly
elegant mansions multiply,
so it's rather like walking
through the pictures in a calendar.
Most of these houses
with their huge watch-dogs
have no name-plate at the door
and are always quite empty.
Maybe their owners spend the whole day
earning money out on the market-place,
shedding their blood on the battle-field,
defending their own money and strength.
They seem to have no time to come home.
What a waste these big empty houses.
Of course the people who work at home
never have this kind of house.
What you call a house may be small
but it must have a roof to keep out rain and snow
and walls that are wind-proof.
Yet the people who actually live in houses
have nothing that really keeps out the weather;
when the roof leaks in the rainy season
they arrange buckets here and there on the floor
and get through the summer.
When the wind comes in through cracks in the wall
they put on more clothes
and get through the winter,
fighting off the fumes from the coal-briquettes.
Even without any garden or gateway,
messy smelly shacks
bring life to bustling alleys.
If you go up the road over Bukhan hill
with its wide asphalt surface,

gloomy mansions multiply
where nobody is admiring the beautiful view,
nobody breathing the fresh breeze,
nobody listening to the sound of birds and streams,
so it's like passing through the Village of Death.

In Those Days

Was there anyone who didn't know?
What everyone felt.
What everyone went through.
Was there anyone who didn't know?

In those days
everybody knew
but pretended not to know.
What no one could say,
what no one could write,
was spoken
in our language,
written in our alphabet
and communicated

Was there anyone who didn't know?
Do not speak too glibly now times have changed.
Stop and think.
In those days,
what did you do?

Bones

When I saw on an X-ray film
the bones that hold up my body,
they seemed not at all to be mine.
The fractured rib was not
made of stainless steel
or of plastic
but neither was it the rafters
of a God-given soul.

Dust of anchovies and eels
piling up over a few dozen years,
hardening and growing into bones
that I have never once seen
and have taken too much for granted.
Everything made of dust,
gathered together and hardened,
sometime or other cracks, breaks
and is finally smashed back into dust.

The bones that hold up my body too
will turn at last to dust
and after drifting like snow-flakes through space
will one day pile up again.
My fractured rib too,
sometime or other will twirl
here and there as dust no longer mine
and be quite unable to remember anything
of my pain.

These bones will break and leave me.
In the bustling market and streets too
no one stays very long.
All hurry past and vanish
and between the gaunt but lingering trees
the wind comes blowing.
It too belongs to no one.

Familiar Shoes

Today a pair of shoes is lying
in front of the door of apartment 1301.
The heels are worn down slantwise,
the toes scuffed pale.
Those old shoes are undoubtedly
the ones he wore.
Who knows perhaps when he was young
he slaved in the fields
to bring up his family.
After losing his old wife
he was obliged to leave his village
and finally ended up in his son's home.
So he came to live silently,
secluded like a criminal in a room
in New Town's high-rise apartment blocks.
His grandchildren said he smelt and disliked him;
his daughter-in-law found doing his washing a bind;
his son was busy so they never met.
Every night he watched the television through to the end.
Each morning, going up the nearby hill,
he would count the notes in his wallet
and examine his Farmers' Cooperative Savings Book.
During the day he would stare down
from the veranda on the 13th floor
like a skinny animal trapped in a cage.
If he encountered anyone in the elevator
he would quickly turn his gaze aside
and say nothing.
He must have lived here about ten months
and we never once exchanged a greeting
but today his familiar shoes
are lying outside the door of 1301.

A Good Son

That friend of mine
lived with his widowed mother beyond middle age.
Now his hair is graying.

Today he and his wife have come out shopping,
he with a mourning badge for his mother
fixed to his lapel, and together
they are choosing a tie.

Since those two got married
I have never seen them look so carefree
and so cheerful!

An Old Pine Tree

Old pine tree,
under a preservation order
in the garden in front of the Saemaul Center—
you have been standing there unchanging
for a good hundred years now,
casting your cool shade
and showing the movement of the breeze.
Judging by your trunk where even the resin has dried up,
your roots must have got diseased
but the people here,
having no idea of how weary you feel,
have enclosed your lower trunk in cement
and even given you injections,
telling you to just keep on standing there.
It may not be at all desirable
but nothing is more natural than old age
and how you must wish after such a long time
just once to flop down and take a rest.
Of course, several centuries may pass
before you rise again after resting
but who can dispel your drowsiness?
Well look at that! Finally closing your green eyes
after keeping them open for a century or more
you have fallen asleep standing up,
old pine tree
with your drooping red branches.

Mountain Heart

Since I cannot be born again,
on days when my heart grows grim
I leave my quiet house
and go away to the mountains.
If I climb to the top of K'ŭnak Mountain,
leaving the world to its own devices,
with only scattered rocks and dense foliage
between the leaves of the dark-hooded oaks,
a wild cat slinking past
on a rotting tree stump,
a lizard basking in the sun,
jealous of all these trees and animals
that have the earth and the sky for their home,
living at ease with just their bare bodies,
and of those flowers and insects
that die and are reborn year by year,
I let loose a heroic cry: "Yahoo!"
But since there is no Lord of the mountain,
all I get back is a wayfaring voice.
I may climb the lofty peaks
or go down into the deep ravines,
the mountain has no central point,
only everywhere the chirping of mountain birds
mingles and flows with the foaming torrents,
while the scent of the dark green forest
unfolds and rises cool.
Unable to settle gently on a branch,
unable to sleep huddled in a rocky crevice,
unable to rot away with the dead leaves,
leaving behind my heart
that longs to live in the mountains,
I depart and
on the day I return from K'ŭnak Mountain,
now a nameless little hill,
in house and village
I am reborn.

Like Someone Fussing and Fretting
(1988)

Gazing Up Into a Persimmon Tree

All the leaves have fallen,
only the fruits remain, ripe and red.

How beautiful!
How tasty they must be!

Banishing all such thoughts,
how about just gazing for a long while
blankly
up into the persimmon tree?

Instead of speeding along
briefly glancing once
quickly snapping a picture, then
dashing away again—
how about staying here, standing or sitting,
bewitched,
lost in thought,
gazing up into the persimmon tree?

We too becoming part of winter's family
for just a little while . . .

Snails' Love

On the mossy cement
of the yard in front of the storage terrace
two snails
are rubbing faces.

To crawl this far
they traversed deafening thunderstorms
and rain solid as bamboo poles –
I wonder how long it took.

Perhaps they came racing along,
abandoning their bodies to longing while still far apart.
They hastened panting along
calling one another with inaudible names
at motionless speed
and now they have joined their bodies
and are whispering endless sweet nothings of love.

I struggled fourteen years
to acquire a tiny house
to contain my brief love—
how remote from me, how enduring
snails' love must be,
for they have a house from the day they're born.

Evening Snow

Waiting for trams
at open air stops
on winter evenings we
longed to become houses for one another.
We longed to become snug rooms
inside which
every kind of shame could be concealed.
Snow might fall
and wind might blow—
we longed to become enclosing walls for one another
until day dawned.

Like Someone Fussing and Fretting

As I left the bank after withdrawing
some small change, the icy wind
ruffled my hair.
The image of that dignified borrower
sitting in the lending clerk's reception area—
there was no way I could pass through Shinch'on
without treading on ground belonging to him.
The sidewalk glistening with artificial marble
was disfigured by messy blobs of gum.
Beneath the street, subway trains were speeding.
Below them again subterranean rivers flowed
and at levels lower still
rocks in flames were burning crimson.
At least I'm lucky to have been born
in a country free of earthquakes.
In a corner of this globe
with five billion people living on it,
one slice of Seoul
where ten million citizens swarm:
that piece of land, that will not fit
into any safe, had been the possession
of that real estate broker. He had freely
conveyed it, mortgaged it, sold it
while I had floundered about on it
working all day long
in order to earn some small change
that I spent my life carefully hoarding,
fussing and fretting.

Smithy Temptations

Sometimes I feel like a plastic object
not made with my own hands
but bought cheaply ready-made,
used carelessly and
thrown out once it breaks.
At such moments I feel I want to jump straight off the bus
and go in search of Hairy's smithy
that vanished from Hŭngŭn-dong crossroads
when Hyŏndae Apartments went up.
To be heated like a bar of pig iron
in a fire made incandescent by blasts from the bellows,
forged on the block,
sharpened on a whetstone—
I feel I want to turn into a sharp, cast-iron sickle.
Becoming a curved hoe,
made one after another, beaten out with sweat running down,
I want to be hung on the smithy wall
with resin oozing from a pinewood handle.
When I grow full of shame
at my life hitherto—
when I feel like a lump of shit
falling into the distant depths
of the old-style privy at Chikji Temple—
I stop in my tracks and suddenly
feel I would like to be hung up somewhere.

Words Dad Left Behind

There's no need to be upset
when you say that Dad's suddenly vanished.
Saying that Dad is no longer beside you
does not make the world any different.
You just have to watch your words as ever
and be sure to keep the door locked even by day.
Let people know you can't accept the invitation for tomorrow
and notify them that you won't be able
to attend the military training the day after.
Saturday is Ma's birthday—
be sure to buy a cake and wish her a happy birthday.
The last day of the month's the day for offerings—
the anniversary of your grandfather's death.
I've already written out the prayer
so celebrate the offerings together.
It will be better to bring the potted plants indoors
before the weather gets any colder.
There's no need to be sad,
even though Dad won't be coming back again.
It's not so long before you'll be a Dad
then your daughter will become a Ma
and have a son like his father
or a daughter like her mother
living in the same house in some neighborhood
unchanging, just like now
so when you say a few people have vanished,
it doesn't make the world any different.

North South East West

In spring a flood of tender green goes rising,
spreading northward, northward.
Unhindered by barbed wire or military demarcation line
it journeys north.
Rising over mountains
crossing plains,
azaleas and forsythias cross the border north.
In summer the cuckoo's call,
the croak of frogs,
are just the same in every place.
In fall a flood of golden hues comes dropping
spreading southward, southward.
Unhindered by demilitarized zone or lines forbidding access
it journeys south.
Crossing rivers
passing over valleys
cosmos flowers and crimson leaves cross the border south.
In winter the taste of ice-cold pickle
the taste of spicy morning soup
are just the same in every place.
North South East West: making no distinction,
covering everywhere alike
in white, no one can keep back
the snowstorm.

At the Back of a Temple Hall

Up the stone steps of the temple behind Mount K'ŭnak
echo sounds of wooden blocks and chanting;
taking a sip of spring water
instead of bowing before Buddha,
I cross the ancient courtyard
patterned by strokes of a brushwood broom.
Behind the main hall a faded
white cow grazes beneath the eaves
broken roof-tiles lie scattered
a paper pagoda left from last Buddha's Birthday—
a shady place like a shed down some back-alley—
someone seems to be there;
as I pause the fern leaves
tremble, vanishing signs
and the rear view of one never once seen
briefly touch my heart.

It was a kind of changing room.

Everyone was standing naked and empty-handed before the door.

Mr. A's face was the first I noticed—he's often in the newspapers. It looked very odd for him to be standing there alone naked—he'd always gone around carrying a gun under his arm, directing his subordinates to haul away citizens.

Mr. B was there too. He owned vast tracts of land, numerous high buildings, and a private plane. But standing there without any escort, naked, he looked really seedy.

One ludicrously obese fellow standing in a corner looked familiar. It was Mr. C—always rigged out in the latest fashion, he used to slide on and off the television screen. On his naked bottom he had a huge birthmark.

Street-cleaner Mr. D was smiling quietly.

Dressed in dark clothes with a bright orange jacket, he used to collect stinking trash early every morning. Now he'd stripped off his working clothes and was standing there at his ease; his body, strengthened by hard work, was quite pleasing to the eye.

The first to be summoned was Mr. A. He passed confidently through the door, swinging his shoulders. Then a sudden scream rang out. Nobody had ever heard a scream like his.

Mr. B followed, going in after pacing up and down looking apprehensive and impatient. He too uttered a single cry. He had never once in all his born days uttered such a sound.

Mr. C, seized with fear, tried to dash outside and was caught. Roughly dragged back, as he went in he was wriggling like a mouse caught by the tail.

Surprisingly, Mr. D was politely escorted in through the door. His voice could be heard from inside, humble as when he used to come to collect the cleaning fee.

There was no way I could find out what on earth was going on behind that door.

Swallowing nervously with a dry throat, I waited before the door for my turn to come.

Aniri
(1990)

In Front of That House

With an earphone stuck in his ear
carrying a walky-talky in one hand
a gas mask slung at his side
come rain come snow
for two and a half years
he stood in front of that house.
In earlier times a famous general lived there
a solid romanesque style mansion that
at one point was the property of the nation
but now it's empty
and guarding that house
for two and a half years
come rain come snow
standing at the foot of the alley
dressed in plain clothes
he fulfilled his military duty
to defend the homeland.

Aniri 1

Do you remember?
How once all the leaves had fallen
the defiant oaks were
standing like ghosts?
On the day the snow melted
the southern plains
slowly undressing before our eyes?
The Imjin River frozen solid
looking at times like a corpse?

Preserved all winter long, those candid hours
have vanished without a trace
and now we are trying to hide them.
We are trying to cover them over.
The faintly drifting scent of springtime grass
the breeze over the fields blowing faintly green
the sound of the river murmuring

languidly flowing—are we going to be
deceived again?
are we going to fall victim
to spring as it yearly returns?
The fickle seasons quickly change
as we merely wait
for proud lonely winter to come again

Summer Trees

Despite the spring drought
the summer trees bloom, develop leaves
assiduously even bear fruit—
at last long-awaited rain falls
and washes them clean.
The evergreen needles of pine trees
the sparkling leaves of jujube trees—
it washes them all without exception.
Even the branches, thick with pale dust
it washes refreshingly.
Rain pours down like bamboo poles
to comfort the trees that cannot wash themselves.
Waves endlessly race toward the shore
in search of trees that cannot swim
calling to the sky
calling to the sea
with the sound of birds, crickets, and wind
the summer trees wave dark green hands.

A Zelkova Roof

Abruptly it grew dark as midnight. Following a flash of lightning there came a sound like some great tree-trunk crashing down onto a tarred road and it began to rain drops as big as grains of corn. For almost an hour it poured down, the proverbial cats and dogs.

In every house the roofs leaked, water poured into the cellars, embankments collapsed on all sides, burying outhouses, drains were blocked so the roads flooded, rivers overflowed and carried away whole fields. Even in houses the water did not enter, the furnishings and equipment all grew damp and soggy.

The one exception was the space beneath the spreading tree at the center of the village.

Underneath that huge tree, reputed to be over a hundred years old, the village elders would play chess and paduk in summer. Around the base of the trunk, which measured more than two spans round, there was a low embankment of piled stones where children used to play games and read comics.

Amazingly, that remained completely untouched by the rain. It was so dry that dust would still blow up from the ground.

I had known from long since that the zelkova cast a thick shadow but I could never have imagined that all those leaves together could serve so effectively as a roof.

Early Winter

I expect I'll soon get used to living alone.
There'll be no news from the children studying abroad,
tax demands will be the only things fluttering in.
Striking up friendships with other solitary birds,
maybe I'll start going to church.
Saying early morning prayers,
listening hard to sermons,
happy to be praised by the priest,
running about all day long helping people, I expect
I'll collapse exhausted and forget each day that passes.
After selling the old house
with the hill behind where nightingales sang
I'll finally move into an apartment
then just when the heating charges go up
I expect I'll find myself laid up with back problems.
Sleep forgotten
deprived of dreams
responding with tears to bright smiles,
I expect I'll get used to being sick alone.
And I suppose I'll wait for the days ahead
that no one can ever get used to.
I'll wait for that long future, I suppose.

A Tune With the Slowest Rhythm

First delicately trembling
then boldly ringing out
and in the gap between trembling and ringing
there is a brief pause.
And between one line and the next
that silence too
like the spaces left white in oriental ink paintings
yielding a sound that can be heard

Dragon Mountain Temple

The smoke of slow incense invoking love and blessings
first seared various gods black
then the fire of money burning
drifting above the roof
turned into a dragon.
Engulfing the wind
seizing hold of the clouds
it seemed about to rise straight to heaven
on account of the fervent hopes
twisting above the roof-ridge
it cannot look down on this temple
from the high windows of its palace.
It has to look upward.

Birds Feeding

As the back door creaks open
it's as if the housewife had called them—
birds fly whirring down
and gobble remains of food
in the garbage area beneath the paulownia.
The magpies like bits of mackerel,
pigeons gobble the tops of bean-sprouts
and sparrows glean grains of rice.
They don't clamor boisterously
don't fight over the food.
As soon as a feeding session is over
with a whoosh of their wings
they fly up to perch on eaves or branches
preening their feathers with their beaks
or chatter together.
They do not peck at one another's sore spots.
The birds consort together naturally
and occasionally peep
from outside the bird cage
or rather, outside the window
into the bird cage
or rather, into our house.

Aniri 8

When we wore father's old clothes cut down to size
and spent winter nights gnawing peeled cabbage roots,
our younger siblings with their close-cropped heads grew strong
and our older sisters enjoyed dates in Sajik Park.
There was nothing to be ashamed of.
Poverty was conscience
and the wealth of us all.
Sons and daughters,
who've sold that last treasure
to buy videos and air cons and sports-cars:
What need is there for you to hide your faces
under that thick make-up,
somehow feeling ashamed, perhaps,
disguise yourselves as film-stars or singers,
play the stock market?
What you need to recover,
dear daughters-in-law and sons-in-law,
is not the treasure your parents bequeathed,
it's the poverty you've forgotten.

Workers' Day

Today the car-park is completely empty.
The parking attendant has not come to work.
All day long the sunshine streams down
on the open space, stained with splashes of oil;
from time to time pigeons come in search of food,
the wind blows past.
With no sign of people working,
no trace of things left lying around,
empty, open to the sky, this patch of ground
has thrown off every unjust occupier
and for a moment reclaimed its rights
as it enjoys its rest; today let's not call
this open space a car-park.

That Person

All my struggles were of no avail.
With nowhere to set my feet,
nothing to catch hold of,
swept away by the waves,
just flailing—
the swimming champion who had come with me
and the sturdy life guards were all of no use.
The shore was fading into the distance
and every shape was vanishing under water.
Just when it all depended entirely on me
and I'd concluded that the sea would be the end of me,
someone threw me a life-belt.
But I don't know
who that person was.
I go on living, not knowing.
But when the world weighs down on me
and I conclude that things will go on just the same
and finally be the end of me
I remember again
that person
who threw me the life-belt—
that person,
I don't know who it was
but I reckon that the world is full
of people just like that.

Waterways
(1994)

No More Elder Brothers

An older friend I wanted to trust like a brother,
a friend I wanted to stay up all night talking to,
a younger friend I wanted to care for like a son—
in the old days such friends existed.
Eyes full of laughter,
a draft of warm water—
in the old days such things existed
but now they all have to be paid for,
with no credit given, either.
Alone after paying the bill
a viaduct carrying the subway above my head,
vanishing into the darkness
where black drops of water fall,
that fellow with his flow of incomprehensible nonsense,
familiar face, rounded shoulders—
I see him daily in the glass—
myself, turned into that elder brother.

Nothing Left But Fire?

The clear waters of Ch'ongye Stream,
have disappeared from the maps of Seoul,
covered with reinforced concrete,
while the rich fields and old Hanyang's earthy smell
all evaporated long ago.
While the Naktong River, descended from heaven,
has completely transformed its lengthy stream
so that now the billowing grace of its flowing waters
stinks to heaven as it makes its way down
and sticky fear alone pools black
like oil.
Is fire the only thing left to us?
Then as now, unchanging everywhere,
is fire the only thing that burns?
Bonfire or gas fire, it makes no difference,
the flame goes blazing upward;
in virgin forest or high-rise apartment blocks,
fire burns everything.
Is fire all we've got left? Fire
that can burn,
drying up and driving out without trace
the water that kept us alive,
and even turning our bodies to charcoal?

A Slide

In the shantytown's playground, snot-nosed kids
are busy playing on a slide.
Storming up the steps of the slide
they come swooshing down again.
All day long from morning to night
you play on the slide
until the seats of your pants wear out.
Why you keep on sliding down?
No one ever asks.

High up in the distant Alps,
people climb to near the Matterhorn
then go irresistibly sliding
down dazzling white sheets of ice.
Skiers thronging from all over the world,
all sorts of little folk playing about
look far smaller than any ant
on the broad breast of fathers soaring aloft
in the gentle embrace of mothers flowing down.
You all go sliding fearlessly
down steep snowy slopes.
Why do you keep on sliding down?
No one ever asks.

His Given Role

He performed his role well.
Sine he was playing the villain,
there was no need to hate him.
The audience enjoyed the play
and when the curtain fell
they applauded as if they wanted to bring the house down.
Leaving the stage,
he removed his makeup
changed into his scruffy everyday clothes
emerged through the stage door and
went back home.
A role that no one gave him
is waiting for him.
No interval,
no knowing when it will end,
no one applauding
he mounts the stage once again
for his weary main role.

An Empty Space

Setting off in a cloud of black smoke
the hearse crossed the bridge
paused for a moment then, when the green arrow appeared
turned left and moved away
westward.
So this morning he finally left
the neighborhood
he had lived in for sixty-three years.
Tormented by hardship and loneliness,
thin as a dead branch of wood, the old man
has abruptly vanished,
leaving behind an incredibly large empty space.
If that space is to be filled, in the coming time
a lot of people are going to have to have their hearts toss and turn
unable to sleep,
weeping in secret.

Welcoming Autumn

The September sky grows higher each day,
full of swarms of dragonflies busily mating
while tingling sunlight ripens maize in hillside fields
and rush mats feel chill in the evenings.
Cicadas, their faces covered
with the withered leaves of
persimmon trees and weeping willows
that are losing their luster,
under the fronds of ivy and the thistle forests
grasshoppers and insects
are all in full cry
all day long.
They seem intent on weeping in utter abandon before they go,
expressing the grief they have been storing up throughout the summer
or singing completely to the very last note
the songs of grief lodged within them.
They seem intent on filling their wide open shells with autumn
before leaving them behind.

Song of an Oak Tree

The shadow cast by the oak tree grows fainter
as autumn passes
countless, a host of leaves
have ceased to cling to the tree
not one remains
all are falling. And now, like those leaves
flying off in a host of hues
with no trace of regret to low-lying places,
I too long to fall quickly
but not onto asphalt, I don't like that
and not onto a flat concrete roof, I wouldn't like that
rather I long to join a pile up in a valley or out in a field
but since I still have such feelings, I'm still
a long way from becoming like a leaf
and living like an oak leaf was a mistaken idea.

A Tropical Bird

Waiting until the lions have eaten their fill
then a mob of hyenas and vultures have torn and devoured
the rest of the zebra's bloody carcass
and flies, or ants
have abolished completely the remaining skin and bones
until the sun sets over the savannah
and the moon rises above the jungle,
its heavy tail drooping
all through the unbearably sultry day
its graceful form perched on a branch
enduring, watching
indeed spending its entire life
in watching thus—
one tropical bird. . .

High Mountain

Mountain, like a watercolor of a spring day
like a dark green botanic garden in summer
deep mountain, that can't be entered by driving a car
that can't be scaled by taking a lift, mirror
for young girls just starting to use make-up,
that we try to walk up but with no end in sight
long to just snuggle down in a valley
where one winter's day when snow drifts high
and the paths are blocked
turning into great animals exposing black fur
gathered in herds, curling up snugly. . .

The Millipede and the Cricket

One lengthy millipede
creeping up my leg
ruined my sleep last night
today one huge cricket jumping about
beside my pillow woke me at dawn.
You creepy beasts
spending the winter inside our bedroom
I'm leaving you alone for the moment
but once the snow has melted
and spring breezes start to blow,
be warned, I'll be sweeping you all outside.

The Never Aging Artist

First he applies to his canvas
the deep yellow color of forsythia blossom
or the soft pink of early azaleas
next stealthily changes to a pale green
before rubbing dark green in at random
then when he feels bored uses a variegated maple die
but if none of these colors please him
he covers his entire canvas with white
then rests for a moment
before he starts to paint a new spring.

Nothing of My Own, But Still . . .
(1998)

A Bell

As the verdigris-crusted bronze silence is shattered,
shouts and groans stored up for centuries are restored to life,
then the deep reverberations die away,
seeming to leave behind a greater stillness.

Mutter Mutter

Attention!
All you who with a single word move whole regiments
so that they are prepared to fight to the end!
You who can stir crowds to a frenzy with a husky call
and make them love you—
reassure a trembling heart with a sweet whisper.
One dish of black noodles, two mixed sea-food noodles!
A downward adjustment of the economic growth rate! A total wage freeze!
You'll go to hell if you don't believe in Jesus!
Buy some dried mackerel or a swordfish!
With everyone raising their voices and shouting,
who makes any effort to hear
words gabbled on their own—
mutter mutter?
Yet everywhere you go,
there is nowhere you cannot hear, borne on the wind,
the sound of an endless muttering
and there is no lack of people
who spend their whole lives muttering
so it's hard to understand.
Mutter mutter

The Price of Silence

How's Ma?

(The voice is clear, crossing the miles between remote east Europe and the Far East)

Your Ma can't take the phone now.

. . . .

(There was once a critic who denounced the custom of printing four periods then leaving the rest of the line blank, instead of writing that no one spoke, as an offence against authorial conscience.)

. . . .

Then Ma . . .?

Mm. Everyone has to, some time . . .

I can't believe it.

. . . .

Dad

Yes

. . . .

(For the ensuing forty-five minutes twenty-four seconds of brief snatches of conversation between father and daughter, a few words followed by long silences, after midnight, the telephone bill came to 27,849 Won.

Everyone, sometimes, can only keep silent.

Today, silences can be heard from one side of the globe to the other, but still . . .)

In a Coal-Mining Village

Piles of coal towering higher than the electricity pylons
and between them, up the valley, the mining village,
houses with slate roofs clustered tightly together,
streets too narrow for a handcart to pass
where wild plants are drying
on cement sacks spread on the black ground.
Kids with faces painted Indian-style
scream, hanging from the broken rope of a swing,
the sound of women quarrelling in the cigarette store,
while workmen coming off duty with freshly washed hair
march resolutely down the hill
as if they mean never again to return to that workplace.
I try to walk, holding my breath apologetically
like a tourist who has entered a lepers' colony
but here even my casual shirt,
dirty as it is from the long journey, feels far too white
and as I leave the village, where there is neither host nor guest,
the coal dust penetrating deep into my lungs
weighs down my parting steps.

A Suit With No Pockets

Obliged to go on a long journey, I did well
after all to prepare a suit for the journey
spaciously made, in a good cloth.
But why are there so many pockets
for a journey where there's no need to pay a fare?
A coverlet smartly made and added on
and buttons to fasten it with
an inner pocket to hold a wallet or passport
made so that it can be closed with a zipper,
small and big pockets all added together
came to twenty-three
surely too many, no matter how fashionable?
The crowd following was no special use, either;
after all, if it's a matter of setting off alone empty-handed,
I ask you, what's the point of making the clothes you wear
on that final journey with so many pockets?
A suit without any pockets would do just as well.

The World I Long For

I reckon there may be another world
between this world
and the world beyond.
All kinds of flowers and trees mixed to form a great forest
humans and animals drinking the same water together
earning the money we need
operating easy machines together—
a place where everyone lives on good terms in harmony.
I keep dreaming of such a world
though I have so far never been there
but still I long for it
and I don't know how many times
I have prudently exercised my voting rights,
yet invariably the candidate
I voted for
lost.

Unknown Road

A place nobody's heard of if you ask the way,
beyond the site of initial construction work for a new city,
the old village of Yong-mori, Dragon-head, appeared.
Mugwort sprouting on the roof-ridge of an old tiled house,
glimpses of thatched roofs overgrown with pumpkin stalks;
from the piles of earth where one bald hill had been leveled
a few shards of ancient pots emerged.
Once the last hill and patch of trees are bulldozed away,
the valleys filled with garbage,
an apartment complex like a chess-board will arise here
under which the old village of Yong-mori, Dragon-head,
        will have disappeared.
Passing the house where the brushwood gate creaked in the earthen wall
and rose-moss blossomed on the storage terrace,
the wind that has slowly made its way up the sinuous alley
suddenly screams as it strikes the angle of a high-rise building
and in Yong-tu-shi, Dragon-head City, more and more people
cannot find their own homes after nightfall.
It's a place where no-one answers if you ask the way.

City of Anxieties

A dyke was built to block the current
in one narrow channel that used to
give comfort looking out from afar
at the wide sea, where tides rose and fell every day.
Dry land was formed, the map changed.
The mudflats where crabs and gobies used to lurk have vanished,
the footprints of flocks of seagulls are covered over,
an oil refinery spouts thick smoke, that's all.
A high hill has been quarried, fields created,
even the trees behind the village shrine have been chopped down.
In the apartment complex built out in the plain
there's not one tree for magpies to nest in,
roads and empty lots are covered with cars,
there's not even a playground for the kids.
In the fresh-water lake within the reclaimed area,
oily waste and sewage stagnate,
wrapping the city of anxieties in a sickening stench
while the population will pass the million mark in the near future
and in this place, ignorant of forests, hills and sea,
the teenagers go roaring round on motorbikes,
imitate videos in the empty sheds of abandoned farms,
maybe hammer nails into the ancestral shrines of their forebears
and the price of land gets higher year by year
as cockroaches and parasitic pine-flies increase daily.

Bird Food

The magpie squawking in the persimmon tree
never flies directly down into the garden.
After hesitating a while at the treetop
it shifts his perch to a lower branch
hops briskly down to the thick bough at the very bottom
as if skipping downstairs
then flies down to the bird food bowl.
It cautiously pecks a few times
before flying away.

If a pigeon spots something to eat
from the top of a telegraph pole or the eaves of a house,
with a few flaps of its wings it
flies almost straight downward.
Then it stuffs itself greedily
until the bowl of bird food is empty.
Even if someone comes very near
it won't fly away.

I never see the cat arriving.
When I look out of the window
on hearing the sparrows chirping wildly
there the cat is, shaking its front paws sharply
as it steals the bird food.
Not that there's any need to call it bird food.
It's simply food offered to
any hungry animals.

A Snail's Pace

Intersecting the path through the fir-trees
among which bats keep speeding
one common snail
goes crawling on.
All on its own—
no family
no windows to shut
no front-gate with door-bell attached, of course,
absolutely no house
to look after in life
and no legs
to be retracted inside
or extended outside
advancing at the speed of its unfolding destiny—
one common snail
goes crawling along on itself
eyes lowered
with never a thought
at a snail's pace.

Komi's Hole

Sight and hearing dim
not even able to smell things any more
that once agile back grown bent
his whole body shriveled up
he dwindled away until at last
early this morning he emerged from the house.
As he was forced into
that almost invisible, tiny hole
there was nothing left but his white furry frame.
Those once straight ears drooping lifelessly
eyes open
four legs stretched out peacefully
we buried the dead body under a pine up on the hill.
Over the last thirteen years
our youngest son, that imp, has grown into a private first class
several presidents have come and gone
our once newly built house has aged and worn out
and been rebuilt and lived in, and all that while
Komi on his leash
blinking his eyes
has been fully absorbed
in his quest for that hole.

Archaeopteryx

In the primeval forests of long long ago
even the dinosaurs dragging their thick great tails
had heads as well.
In the trackless level swamps
the reptiles crawling on their bellies
still had their dreams.
Falling, slipping, wailing, after long wandering
rising with front limbs extended
they stared around in all directions
Hanging on, falling off, laboriously
they crawled up onto the branches of trees
and gazed at what lay beyond the hills.
They too had their far-away, lofty places.
Without that, how would they have risen into the sky
and left their dreams of life in fossils?

Buddha Made of Wood

This wooden statue of Buddha from Ubud, Bali,
was bought for just seventy dollars after some hard bargaining
but during the seven hour flight back across the equator
it broke off from its lotus-blossom stand.
The workmanship was so exquisite
it seemed a pity to give it away
so I placed it on my desk.
Placed it there and looked at it.
Was it the quality of the mahogany?
Was it the influence of breathing and looking?
The break suddenly seemed to heal
and now there's no sign of it.
That little brownish-red Buddha
does not seem to be made of wood at all
it's as though it was originally born in the shape of Buddha.
I can't work out what it means but at some point
a little wooden Buddha came into my heart and sat down there.

A Summer Shorter than Expected

That man was once a great wrestler,
at the very center of competitions
with the band tied round his thigh.
Hurling his opponent onto the sand of the ring
then roaring a shout of victory, he
was a famous champion in his youth.
With the acclamations that made the ring tremble behind him now,
who would recognize the elderly muscle man I saw yesterday
disappearing alone up an alley?
Springtime was lovely, but it's over now,
summer was shorter than expected, suddenly
night is falling over deserted plains
and even if he says he'll go walking on,
how will he deal with approaching winter?

A Good-for-Nothing Friend

Close as leeches we certainly were not.
I mean, we did not first meet
on account of any kind of usefulness.
Unable to lend money to cover debts,
no use in promotions and transfers
no way of getting jobs for the children
we have kept company for a long time and he long ago
realized that I was a pretty much good-for-nothing person
while I too came to that conclusion long ago.
Still, he must have sensed long ago that
I was pretending not to know that.
If we meet, we are simply glad
and we'll probably go on living like that—
now we're suddenly both forty-five years old—
each other's pretty much good-for-nothing friend.

For Someone

You always lived for your husband
for your children
for your parents and siblings
or else for the sick in heart and naked in body
for the rejected, for oppressed neighbors,
or simply for others
always indifferent to anything for yourself
and suddenly you went away.
Your bright smiling face
the hollow left where you sat on the grass
the autumn sunlight you used to bask in
the warm sound of your voice
all simply left behind
you vanished, alone, in a flash.
You turned into water and crossed the Han River
you turned into a cloud and floated over the peak of Pukhan Mountain
you went flying away in a north-westerly direction—
you may have become a wind flattening the grass on a Mongolian steppe
or you may have become a star gazing down by night on dark roofs
or have you become a mist
snugly enveloping us all?
Did I sometime simply look at you?
Did we merely send you off?
Clearing out the clothes you used to wear,
withdrawing from the bank the money you left behind
walking along the streets you used to go along
it feels as if one day or other you will reappear
so we keep looking behind us.
Only now, missing you immensely, are we
trying to change gradually? Is each of us
trying silently to become more like you?

From Seoul to Sŏkch'o

When we drove that long distance from Seoul to Sŏkch'o
she was sitting there beside me.
It was a mistake to go speeding on, only staring ahead.
I should have turned my eyes aside now and then and looked
at her with the North Han River or Mount Sŏrak for background.
Silence is not necessarily a virtue . . .
it was a mistake not to share much talk with her during
all those long years we spent together.
No need to stare at one another's face
or exchange extraordinary talk
since we knew one another through and through.
but still, understanding does not necessarily mean loving . . .
But there should have been more times spent
playing at being water spirits beside the sea in summer
or in winter sneaking close when the first snow fell then
slipping a handful of snow down a neck and laughing loud.
At least we should often have traded insults:
the soup's watery, you can't cook and
your wages are too low.
It's all right, that kind of thing's natural, any time
a slightly moist smile of comfort
a bright voice
a gentle touch
memories you cannot embrace
all the things that now have vanished inward.

Someone Who Can Listen

The violent storm that blew up in the night
had blown itself out
and as soon as the eastern sky brightened
the people who had spent the night holding their breath
each and all raised a clamor.
Only he remained silent,
having spent the dreadful night awake with me
not hiding sad things or unfair treatment
listening carefully even to trivial talk
nodding as he listened,
with his usual bright smile
peaceful gaze, quiet voice
large ears and tightly sealed lips.
His familiar face has vanished
I can't grasp his soft hand.
There are people who look like him, everywhere,
but now there's no one
who can listen without saying a word.

When First We Met
(2003)

Over the Hill

Every morning the sun rises
above lofty East Hill
that lies to the east of our neighborhood
while on full-moon evenings
the moon rises there.
Over the hill, in Kamak Vale
they call our East Hill West Hill.
Every evening the sun sets
behind West Hill
and late on full-moon nights
the moon goes down behind it.

Ultimate Questions

Telephones
television sets
audio sets
computers
mobile phones . . .
if they stop working
I'm told I should throw the old one away
and buy a new one
rather than try to repair and go on using it.
I'm told that's cheaper.

Nowadays I'm told
it's no different where people are concerned.

Then, our family
city
workplace
nation
world too . . . does that mean
they can't be repaired?
That they have to be thrown away?

This one and only me, too—
can I throw myself away
and buy a new one?

At the Entrance to a Temple

In front of the gateway to a temple
along a path where all the oak leaves have fallen
at a snack bar under a plastic tent
a young monk is eating a serving of odeng.
He slurps down the soup quickly
like a private on his way back to barracks.
The winter cold comes early up in the hills.
He's not afraid of winter
but it takes strength and vigor
to do Zen meditation.

Opinions About Deserts

In foreign lands processions of camels can be seen crossing vast deserts composed of nothing but sand dunes and rocks, to say nothing of caravans searching for oases, misled by mirages.

One can equally imagine torrential rain just occasionally pouring down, smashing through the dry air, turning the desert into a lake, and leaving traces behind in wadis.

One is obliged to accept the way yellow dust goes flying up from the Gobi Desert, clouds the sky over Seoul, then passing over Tokyo reaches San Francisco—not gladly but as part of nature's dispensation.

Whereas there is no understanding the act of waging war, mobilizing tanks and missiles and planes in a barren land, a desert where not even plants can grow.

There is no understanding the violence that indiscriminately massacres tribes which have endured millennia of poverty, turning large countries into desert-like ruins, all in the name of capturing a single, wily terrorist.

Notes on the Poems

Page 31: The midnight curfew. Until the early 1980s, people were not allowed to be on the streets after midnight, for security reasons. During the hour before then, Seoul's streets were full of people trying to catch a taxi or bus, desperate to get home in time.

Page 32: The April Revolution: In 1960, the students of Seoul took to the streets to demand democratic reforms and the resignation of the corrupt Syngman Rhee regime. When they tried to march on the presidential mansion the army shot and killed hundreds of them. Seoul National University was one of the main centers of these protests. At that time it was located in the neighborhood of Hyehwa-dong, in central Seoul, along the street running south from Hyehwa-dong Rotary, known as University Street (Taehak-ro). A few years later, under the dictatorship of Park Chung-Hee, the university was relocated to its present campus south of Seoul, far from the city center.

Rolled up calendars: Every company in Korea used to print and distribute calendars as a form of publicity and the employees were accustomed to use them as gifts for their friends.

Page 34: This poem was immensely popular during the years of dictatorship and repression, when the media were controlled and censored; the truth had to be discovered in other ways, by careful listening.

Page 35: This poem alludes to the way power was exercised and public opinion controlled in the 1970s and 1980s.

Page 42: This is one of Kim Kwang-Kyu's most celebrated poems. Its baby crab incarnates the longing for freedom of generations of young Koreans, some of whom paid with their lives for their resistance to military brutality.

Page 50: Mount Inwang: This small rocky hill (338m) lies just to the west of the royal palaces on the northern edge of old Seoul. It forms part of the geomantic configuration of hills and rivers that justified the establishment of the new capital in the 14th century. The word "Seoul" is applied to whichever town is currently serving as the capital of Korea. The city now known as Seoul was previously known by a variety of names, of which Hanyang is the most familiar. The poet was born and still lives in a neighborhood on the western side of the hill and in this poem explores the contrasts between past and present.

"Eight million." Seoul today has a far larger population but this poem was written prior to the expansion of the city's boundaries in the 1980s and the great building booms of the past two decades.

Page 51: The bear in question has a white patch on its breast in the shape of a half-moon. In popular mythology, such a bear was transformed into a woman who, marrying the son of the Sky God, gave birth to Tangun, the father of the Korean people.

Page 73: Koryo designates the era in Korean history dating from 918 until 1392. It was marked by a highly developed artistic culture and its celadon pottery with inlaid designs is particularly celebrated.

Page 74: April brings the memory of the 1960 April Revolution. May saw the coup by Park Chung-Hee in 1961 and the coup by Chun Doo-Hwan in 1980, marked by the massacres in Kwangju.

Page 76: This poem can really only be fully understood when it is explained that the Korean word for "wisdom tooth" is "love tooth."

Page 81: This poem was first published in the Spring 2005 edition of the review *Two Lines.*

Page 83: The Korean title of this poem is "Friend from Hyoja-dong." Hyoja-dong is a neighborhood in Seoul. The word "Hyoja" means "model of filial piety," which in traditional Confucian morality was a great virtue. In today's world, the obligation to care for one's elderly parents seems rather to be a burden people are glad to be free of.

Page 85: There is no K'ŭnak Mountain in Korea. The name of this imaginary place resembles Kŭngnak, a Buddhist form of Paradise.

Page 92: Shinch'on is a neighborhood in western Seoul crowded with students busily frequenting bars, shops and restaurants.

Page 95: This poem evokes the way nature ignores the division between North and South Korea, crossing the DMZ that no ordinary human being can cross and clearly indicating that Korea is really a single land.

Page 96: "Wooden blocks." A hollow block of wood in the shape of a stylized fish is beaten in a rapid, regular rhythm by monks while chanting the sutras.

"A faded white cow." A series of paintings found on the side and rear walls of many Buddhist temples depicts the taming of a wild cow (ox) by a child, symbolizing the quest for enlightenment. The first painting shows the cow grazing.

"Buddha's Birthday." This is a popular English term for the festival on the eighth day of the fourth lunar month commemorating the "Coming" of the historical Buddha. On the evening before, or a few days before, this festival a procession passes through the streets of Seoul and other towns that includes many papier-mâché figures and objects, including pagodas that then tend to get dumped at the back of temple halls.

Page 101: All young Korean men are expected to do a lengthy period of military service. Some are drafted into the riot police, one of whose duties may be to guard the private homes of previous presidents, even when they have been sent to prison. A contrite-looking Chun Doo-Hwan once promised to donate all his property to the state.

Page 102: In the traditional sung narrative known as Pansori, there are sections of plain narrative that are simply spoken. These are known as Aniri.

Page 104: Many rural communities in Korea still have a meeting place sheltered by a large tree on the edge of the village that is used as a place for communal recreation.

Paduk is a board game played using black and white pieces. It is often known in the West by its Japanese name "Go."

Page 109: "Sajik Park." There are still very few public parks in Seoul; this former royal shrine was one of the few open spaces open to the public without charge.

Page 116: Ch'ongye Stream is a river which flows through central Seoul. In the 1970s it was covered over to become a major thoroughfare, but it was re-excavated in 2005.

"Hanyang" is an old name for Seoul. Until modern times, much of the land inside the city walls was used for farming.

The Naktong River flows southward through south-eastern Korea, entering the sea near Pusan. It is notoriously heavily polluted.

Page 133: The poem refers to the suit of traditional clothes in unbleached ramie in which the dead of Korea are dressed before they are placed in the coffin for their final journey.

Page 136: The ongoing destruction by reclamation of vast areas of tidal mudflats (wetlands) along the west coast of Korea is an ecological crime of global dimensions that the Korean government seems completely unwilling to restrict.

Page 145: Sŏkch'o is a town on Korea's east coast, a popular tourist destination.

Page 151: Odeng is a cheap snack composed of fish-meal dumplings on a skewer immersed in a bowl of soup.

THE POET

Kim Kwang-Kyu was born in Seoul in 1941 and studied German language and literature at Seoul National University. In 1960, early in his university career, he participated in the demonstrations of the April Revolution that were repressed by a tragic massacre on April 19, which led to the fall of President Syngman Rhee. He later studied for two years in Munich 1972-4. Although he had discovered a talent for writing during his middle and high school days, when his work had been published in school magazines and even won a national prize, he did not begin to write poetry after that until he was in his mid-thirties and had come back from Germany. His first published poems appeared in the review *Munhak kwa chisong* in 1975, the same year in which he published Korean translations of poems by Heinrich Heine and Günter Eich. In 1979 his first volume of poems *The Last Dream to Affect Us (Urirŭl chŏksinŭn majimak kkum)* was published but then virtually suppressed in the political tensions surrounding the assassination of President Park Chung-hee in October that year; a second volume *No, It's Not So (Anida, kŭroch'i ant'a)* followed in 1983, a third *The Heart of K'ŭnaksan (K'ŭnaksan ŭi maŭm)* in 1986, a fourth *Like Someone Fussing and Fretting (Chomp'aengi ch'ŏrŏm)* in 1988. There followed *Aniri* in 1991, *Waterways (Mulkil)* in 1994 and *Nothing of My Own, But Still . . . (Kajin kot hanado ŏpchiman)* in 1998. In 1996, he published *Voices Natural and Disguised (Yuksŏng kwa kasŏng)*, a collection of his essays and articles on a variety of literary topics. His most recent collection of poems, *When First We Met (Ch'ŏŭm mannatŏn ttae)*, was published in 2003 and received that year's Daesan Literary Award for poetry.

Since 1980 he has been a professor in the German department of Hanyang University (Seoul) and he has published translations of 19th century German poems (1980), of poems by Bertolt Brecht (1985), of radio dramas by Günter Eich (1986), and of poems by Günter Eich (1987). He has received a number of major Korean literary prizes for his poetry: in 1981 the first Nokwŏn Literary Award and the fifth Today's Writer Award; in 1984 he received the fourth Kim Su-Yŏng Award. In 1994 he was awarded the Pyonun Literary Prize. In recent years, he has been actively engaged in promoting literary exchanges between Korea and Germany and has given readings of his poetry in numerous cities in Germany, Austria and Switzerland. He has equally given readings in Japan, in the United States, and in Medellin (Colombia) where he read to a crowd of eight thousand. To celebrate Kim Kwang-Kyu's sixtieth birthday, a collection of articles about his work was published in 2001 with the title *Kim Kwang-Kyu: Reading Deeply*, which constitutes the most important source for critical comment on his achievement.

In 1988 the late Kim Young-Moo (Professor of English, Seoul National University) published *Faint Shadows of Old Love (Hǔimihan yetsarang ǔi kǔrimja)*, a selection from Kim Kwang-Kyu's first three volumes of poems, with a critical essay. These were translated by Brother Anthony and were published by Forest Books (London) in 1991 with the title *Faint Shadows of Love*. The volume received the Translation Prize in the Republic of Korea Literary Awards for 1991. A volume of German translations by the poet's wife, Chong Heyong, was published in 1999 and won the same award in 2001. Translations of his work have also recently been made into Spanish and Japanese.

The Translators

Brother Anthony of Taizé

Born in Truro, Cornwall (UK), in 1942, Brother Anthony is a member of the monastic Community of Taizé, France. He came to Korea in 1980, and lives in Seoul with other members of the Community. He teaches English literature at Sogang University (Seoul). He has published many volumes of translations of modern Korean poetry, including work by Ku Sang, Sŏ Chŏng-Ju, Ko Un, Chŏn Sang-Pyŏng, Shin Kyŏng-Nim, Kim Su-Yŏng, Lee Si-Yŏng, and others as well as of works of Korean fiction by Yi Mun-Yol and Lee Oyoung. A naturalized Korean citizen, his Korean name is An Sŏnjae.

Kim Young-Moo

Kim Young-Moo was born in 1944 in Paju, near Seoul. After earning his B.A. and M.A. from the English Department of Seoul National University, he received his Ph.D. from the English Department of SUNY at Stony Brook. He became a professor in the Department of English Language and Literature at Seoul National University in 1982. He died in 2001. He published three volumes of poetry as well as volumes of literary criticism, personal essays, and literary translations into Korean. He and Brother Anthony collaborated in translating many of the writers listed above.

The Korean Voices Series